Original title:
Laughs in the Laurel

Copyright © 2025 Creative Arts Management OÜ
All rights reserved.

Author: Juliette Kensington
ISBN HARDBACK: 978-1-80567-325-5
ISBN PAPERBACK: 978-1-80567-624-9

The Orchestra of Nature's Nuances

In the meadow, giggles play,
As daisies dance, come what may.
The butterflies, in colors bright,
Make the sunlight feel just right.

Squirrels chatter, minds at ease,
Tickled by the playful breeze.
The brook hums a merry tune,
While frogs croak 'neath the bright full moon.

Nestled nests of birds up high,
Twirling tales of joy, oh my!
A symphony of silly sights,
As shadows stretch to claim the nights.

Each rustle's filled with joyous calls,
Even the raindrops have their brawls.
Nature's band, what a delight,
Bringing giggles with all its might!

Harmonious Hoots Beneath the Sky

In a tree where owls sing,
Chirping tales that make hearts swing.
Feathers fluff with giggly cheer,
Underneath the stars quite near.

Squirrels dance with little prance,
Join the fun in a wild chance.
A moonlit night with joyful sounds,
As laughter twirls and spins around.

Riddles and Roses in the Air

A bloom whispers secrets wide,
Each petal holds a riddle inside.
Bumblebees buzz in playful chase,
Dancing lightly, setting the pace.

Come, solve the puzzles of delight,
In gardens where imaginations take flight.
With every twist, a chuckle grows,
In fields where the wittiest humor flows.

Breaking Boundaries with Bliss

Flip the rules, let laughter break,
On the pond, the frogs awake.
Splashing joy on lily pads,
Every croak makes the gladness rad.

Chasing shadows of the day,
Joyful chaos leads the way.
With leaps and bounds through every thrill,
We find smiles hidden, ready to spill.

Goofiness of the Grove

In the grove where mischief reigns,
Fooling about, bringing no pains.
Bouncing branches, giggles ring,
Nature joins in the antics they bring.

Each rustle tells a jolly tale,
As critters hop and set their sail.
With every prank a fresh delight,
The grove is alive with laughter's light.

Witty Whispers Among the Vines

In the garden, stems entwine,
Where jokes blossom, oh so fine.
Beneath the leaves, a chuckle stirs,
Nature's humor softly purrs.

Twisting tendrils play their part,
Creating smiles, a work of art.
The sunbeams giggle, shadows play,
In the green, we find our sway.

A Ballet of Glee in the Wild

Squirrels twirl with graceful flair,
Dancing lightly in the air.
Nature's stage, they leap and swing,
A jolly tune is what they bring.

The flowers sway, they join the fun,
In bright costumes, one by one.
With every rustle, laughter swells,
In this wild realm, joy dwells.

The Gentle Giggle of Growing Things

Sprouts arise with playful zest,
Cracking jokes when they're at rest.
Petals flutter, a breezy laugh,
Each little bud, a happy staff.

Roots tickle where they intertwine,
In soft whispers, they align.
The earth below has secrets sweet,
With every pulse, they dance to beat.

Comforting Carols from the Green Sanctuary

In the shade, the crickets sing,
Harmonies that twist and cling.
Leaves rustle softly, tell their tales,
Echoes burst like gentle gales.

Amidst the ferns, a merry sound,
In every corner, joy is found.
Nature's choir, a welcoming cheer,
Playing notes that draw us near.

Tales Told with a Twinkle

In shadows where giggles dwell,
A riddle spins its merry spell.
The cat in socks, a wanderer bold,
Tells secrets that never get old.

A hat thought lost, on a dog's head,
Chasing its tale, where laughter's spread.
The moon winks down, a sly little chap,
As we dance in joy, no need for a map.

Witty Whispers Underneath the Stars

Beneath the sky, a chuckle glows,
A starlet falls, and everybody knows.
The bench that squeaks sings silly tunes,
While owls giggle, sharing their moons.

A jester's hat with bells that cling,
Tells tales of mischief, a jolly fling.
The wind carries jokes from tree to tree,
As crickets join in, a symphony free.

Heartstrings Strummed by Happiness

With laughter strummed on heartstrings bright,
A squirrel dances in morning light.
Chasing its tail, round and round,
While flowers chuckle, joy unbound.

Each slip and trip, a comic art,
As gnomes with grins play their part.
A teapot whistles a hearty cheer,
With every tune, the fun draws near.

Bliss Among the Blossoms

In gardens where giggles sprout and grow,
Petals sway to the humor flow.
A bee in shades plays the fool,
With nectar dreams, it leaves the school.

Butterflies, fluttering with a grin,
Whisper secrets of the joy within.
In every bloom, a story spun,
Where bliss finds roots, and life feels fun.

Grins from the Garden

In the garden where sunflowers sway,
Bumblebees dance in a merry ballet.
Worms wear hats made of leafy green,
Telling tales of the sights they've seen.

Petunias giggle, roses turn bright,
A toad croaks jokes in the soft twilight.
Each bloom offers a chuckle or two,
While daisies whisper secrets anew.

Lively Chatter in the Canopy

In the trees where the squirrels play,
Chirping birds share quips all day.
Branches sway with a joyous laugh,
Each rustle seems a comical path.

The leaves gossip in a soft breeze,
A woodpecker raps on the old trees.
They swap tales of a bright acorn,
While sunlight paints the scene more worn.

Blissful Banter Beneath the Boughs

Under the shade of the old oak tree,
Crickets chirp in harmony free.
A rabbit jokes about his long ears,
As laughter dances, erasing fears.

The shadows tickle the meadow's floor,
While butterflies flit, seeking out more.
Every moment is filled with delight,
As day turns to dusk with stars in sight.

The Art of Joyful Whispers

In the cool glen where ferns unfold,
Whispers weave tales that never grow old.
A chipmunk grins, sharing a jest,
While fireflies glow, lighting the fest.

Moss carpets giggles, soft as a dream,
While the brook chuckles, a bubbling stream.
Nature's laughter, a playful tune,
As day meets night beneath the moon.

Jests in the Jungle

A monkey swings with a silly grin,
He trips on a vine, and starts to spin.
The parrot squawks with bright delight,
As the leopard laughs at the comical sight.

In the midst of trees, a party breaks,
With giggles and shakes, and funny pranks.
The elephant dances with clumsy flair,
While the toucan throws a colorful air.

Radiant Revelries Above

Clouds drift by like fluffy dreams,
As birds chirp out in playful themes.
The sun peeks through with a cheeky beam,
While butterflies join in the colorful scheme.

Up high in the skies, the kites take flight,
Twisting and turning in pure delight.
Laughter resounds from the hilltops near,
As the wind carries joy for all to hear.

Humorous Hues of Harmony

A rainbow stretches in the sky so wide,
Colors mix and swirl with joyous pride.
Each shade giggles and twirls around,
Painting smiles on faces all around.

In gardens bright, the flowers cheer,
As bees dance close, bringing sweet good cheer.
The breeze tickles petals, a light-hearted tease,
While ladybugs join in, moving with ease.

Frolics in the Forest

In the shady glen, where sunlight beams,
Squirrels chatter with silly schemes.
The rabbits hop with laughter so loud,
As the wildflowers nod, all swaying proud.

Frogs leap from lily pads with glee,
Creating ripples as they splish and spree.
The forest echoes with mirthful sound,
Where joy and laughter are always found.

Chuckles in the Sunlight

The sun shines bright with a playful grin,
As giggles dance on the frolicking wind.
Squirrels wear hats, oh what a sight,
While daisies sway in sheer delight.

A butterfly cracks a silly joke,
While a toad leaps forward, puffing smoke.
Under a tree, laughter takes flight,
In a world where everything feels just right.

Smiling Sprouts of Spruce

Tiny sprouts in a comedic parade,
Wobble and giggle, never afraid.
A wise old owl tells tales of the past,
While the mischievous bunnies race fast.

Sunflowers rock in a carnival sway,
As laughter spreads like sprinkles of hay.
Nature's own jesters, in shades of green,
Creating a scene that's joyous and keen.

Gleeful Meanderings Amidst Moss

Amidst soft moss, where the giggles grow,
Playful gnomes scatter mischief below.
Frogs wear bow ties, singing a tune,
While mushrooms bounce like a funny cartoon.

Dancing leaves whisper, secrets they keep,
As squirrels share stories that tickle our sleep.
Each step brings jests, with twinkling eyes,
In this forest where humor never dies.

Breezy Chuckles in the Grove

In the grove where the breezes twist and turn,
The laughter of branches makes our hearts yearn.
Chasing shadows, the playful winds swirl,
As daisies pop out in a joyful twirl.

A family of pixies in jolly delight,
Play tag with clouds, in fluffy white.
Each chuckle is a note in a symphonic spree,
In this delightful world, we all long to be.

Joyful Echoes in the Grove

In the woods where giggles play,
Trees shake softly, come what may.
Squirrels chatter, dance with glee,
Nature's jesters, wild and free.

Fluffy clouds in skies above,
Whisper secrets, tales of love.
Sunbeams tickle every face,
In this bright and happy place.

Birds sing tunes both weird and fun,
Racing shadows as they run.
Breezes carry laughter light,
Twirling leaves in sheer delight.

Every creature joins the show,
With a wiggle and a bow.
In the grove, joy takes its wing,
Hear the chorus as they sing.

Chortles Among the Leaves

Rustling leaves begin to snicker,
The world turns bright, hearts grow thicker.
Playful whispers tease the air,
Funny faces everywhere.

Beneath the branches, giggles swell,
Nature's tale, a jovial spell.
Worms in top hats, ants in shoes,
Each new sight brings hearty news.

A frog croaks jokes, a wise old sage,
Trees clap hands, release the rage.
Mice in coats play hide and seek,
While chirping crickets softly speak.

Every twist, a quirky jest,
In this haven, we're all blessed.
From sunrise till the stars ignite,
Laughter echoes through the night.

Delight in Nature's Embrace

When daisies dance on breezy days,
And butterflies join in the plays.
Cheerful sounds float from afar,
Each ticklish breeze, a shining star.

A squirrel slips on a damp green leaf,
With a tumble and a quick relief.
The brook bubbles with friendly cheer,
As frogs croak jokes for all to hear.

Hummingbirds tease the floral cheer,
Dashing near and then they veer.
In every corner, smiles abound,
Joyful moments, truly found.

Nature chuckles, soft and sweet,
With every skip, our hearts do beat.
In this embrace, we twirl and sway,
Joy will lead us on our way.

Mirth Among the Branches

Oh the games the branches play,
As shadows stretch throughout the day.
With whispered breezes, secrets shared,
In wooded realms, none are scared.

Twirling vines in playful jest,
Invite the birds to join their fest.
Laughter bounces from the tree,
As roots and beams sing merrily.

Pinecones drop with silly thuds,
While raindrops dance in breezy floods.
Every rustle, every sound,
Brings laughter loudly all around.

In the forest, joy takes wing,
Where merry hearts unite and sing.
With every snap and playful tease,
Mirth flows freely, like the breeze.

Nature's Giggle

In the meadow, daisies sway,
Little bugs dance and play.
Whispers of sunshine beam,
Nature's joy, a light-hearted dream.

Squirrels chatter in the trees,
Making mischief with such ease.
Breezes carry laughter's tune,
Bouncing high like a balloon.

Rivers tickle stones along,
Fish leap high in playful song.
Mountains chuckle, absurd and grand,
Nature's wit, an open hand.

With every rustle, giggles rise,
Underneath the vast blue skies.
A world so merry, bright and bold,
Nature's story, sweetly told.

A Jubilee of Joys in the Juniper

Gather 'round the juniper tree,
Where giggles flow so merrily.
Dancing shadows, happy feet,
Every corner, a joyful treat.

Bunnies hop with cheeky flair,
Chasing sunlight, without a care.
The air is thick with glee and fun,
As laughter twinkles in the sun.

Pinecones drop with a playful plop,
As birds chirp and never stop.
Nature beams through every bark,
Filling hearts with a joyful spark.

In the thicket, creatures scheme,
Woven tales that bubble and teem.
A jubilee for every soul,
Harmony makes the spirit whole.

Whimsical Whispers and Woodland Wonders

In the woods, where breezes sigh,
Whispers twirl and spirits fly.
Branches bend to share a jest,
Every rustle feels like a fest.

Foxes grin with sly delight,
Underneath the twinkling light.
Owls hoot in their cozy nooks,
Reading tales from ancient books.

Mushrooms sprout, a colorful show,
Painting paths with a vibrant glow.
Nature's palette, oh so bright,
With laughter spinning through the night.

In this realm of charm and cheer,
Every shadow brings good cheer.
Woodland wonders, playful and sweet,
A magical world where hearts meet.

Serendipity in the Saplings

Tiny leaves, a curious sight,
Stretching up to greet the light.
Swaying softly, oh so free,
   Saplings laugh in jubilee.

Breezes whisper cheeky tales,
  As tiny critters ride the trails.
Every branch has secrets to share,
   Laughter dancing in the air.

In spring's embrace, a joyful dance,
Every moment, given a chance.
Nature winks with playful grace,
In this wild and wondrous place.

With roots that dig and dreams that soar,
  Saplings giggle, wanting more.
Serendipity shines bright and true,
  In this world of green, anew.

The Dance of Dappled Joy

In the sun's warm embrace, they twirl with glee,
Little shadows flit, wild and free.
Beneath the swaying branches, faces aglow,
Giggles burst forth like the flowers that grow.

Silly hats perched atop heads so bright,
Dancing with daisies in the soft twilight.
Whimsical tunes in the breeze take flight,
Echoing laughter till the stars ignite.

Giggles and Greenery: A Tale

In a patch of emerald, where wild things play,
Frogs croak in rhythms, leading the way.
Mice wear their suits made of leaves and twine,
Echoing chuckles that sparkle like wine.

Bumblebees buzz with a joyful cheer,
As they pirouette, no sign of fear.
With a flick and a flap, they sway to the beat,
In this jolly haven, where all friends meet.

The Mirthful Antics of Ivy

Twisting and curling, the ivy will climb,
With playful pranks, it dances with time.
Leaping through gardens, it tickles the rose,
Shiny green tendrils where mischief grows.

Squirrels play tag, in a game of delight,
Chasing their shadows, they bound into night.
Their chatter lifts spirits, oh what a scene,
In this leafy theater where giggles convene.

Sprightly Spirits in the Meadow

In the meadow aglow, where humor ignites,
Fairies play pranks on the comets at night.
With glimmers and sparkles, they frolic and tease,
Winking at mortals who pass by with ease.

Grasshoppers leap in a jovial race,
A carnival spirit spreads joy through the space.
Laughter like music, above the soft breeze,
Whispers of cheer in the gentle tall trees.

Sunshine and Smirks

In a field where giggles bloom,
Sunbeams dance, dispelling gloom.
With each step, a tickle's near,
Laughter's ripples, crystal clear.

Butterflies play tag with bees,
Wandering minds float with the breeze.
A squirrel dons a tiny hat,
And chuckles chase a playful cat.

Jokes sung by the chirping throng,
Echoing like a joyous song.
Even flowers wear a grin,
As the day spins round and round again.

Laughter spills like lemonade,
In this realm where fun won't fade.
With a wink and silly play,
Joyfulness rules the sunny day.

The Heartbeat of Cheerful Sounds

Listen close to the playful hum,
A symphony of joy will come.
Birds in chorus, holding notes,
Their silly tunes, like playful boats.

A drum, a thump, a funny beat,
Where wiggly worms dance on their feet.
Underneath the smiling trees,
Even shadows chuckle in the breeze.

Giggles rise with every breeze,
From blossoms sweet like gentle teas.
A rabbit hops with such delight,
While leaves sway, casting shadows light.

The sun dips low, still jokes unfold,
As twilight whispers stories bold.
In every heart, a spark resides,
For laughter charades where fun abides.

A Symphony of Silliness Under the Trees

Under branches that embrace the sky,
A piper plays a tune nearby.
With notes that tickle every ear,
The woodland creatures gather near.

Rabbits juggle acorns high,
While owls giggle under the sky.
A tortoise skips, a sight so rare,
And even foxes join the affair.

The breeze brings jokes as leaves do sway,
With pie fights in the bright ballet.
Each flower holds a secret joke,
As vines around the laughter choke.

Sunset glows, the laughter flows,
In playful whispers, joy bestows.
With hearts alight, the night unfurls,
A brighter world where fun twirls.

Bursts of Bliss Amidst the Flora

In gardens where the giggles grow,
Petals swirl in the golden glow.
Each bloom bursts with a cheeky grin,
A playful spark in all within.

Bumblebees hum their funny tales,
As wiggling worms don tiny veils.
The daisies bow, the tulips sway,
In a dance that shouts, 'Come play!'

A ladybug in polka dots,
Sprints by, collecting happy thoughts.
While daisies spin and twirl around,
Silliness echoes in joy profound.

With each sunset, the laughter grows,
As flora flutters and sunshine glows.
In this realm, where pleasure's stirred,
Life's sweetest jokes are never blurred.

Joyful Tidings Among the Blossoms

In the garden where giggles bloom,
Petals dance like they're in a room.
Bumblebees hum a silly tune,
Chasing butterflies 'neath the moon.

Daisies wink with a golden eye,
As clouds flip by like popcorn in the sky.
Nature's jesters in bright array,
They juggle the sun in a playful way.

The trees tease with whispers of cheer,
Every rustle brings laughter near.
Frolicsome shadows skip on the ground,
Tickling toes where joy is found.

A chorus of chuckles fills the air,
Each blossom sways without a care.
Join the revelry, let spirits soar,
In this merry land, forevermore.

Mirth in the Meadow

In the meadow, where laughter reigns,
Every blade tells a joke through their chains.
Flowers giggle as they sway,
While grasshoppers leap in a carefree ballet.

Butterflies flit with a wink and a spin,
Kicking up joy with a flip and a grin.
Giggling robins join the show,
Singing sweet nothings as they go.

Clouds above wear silly hats,
Casting shadows that dance like mats.
Sunbeams sparkle with a teasing light,
Painting the field in hues so bright.

With every step, the earth hums a song,
Inviting all to join in along.
So gather 'round and share a laugh,
In this meadow, let's forget the path.

The Lightness of Leisurely Breezes

A zephyr twists with a playful spark,
Carrying giggles through the park.
Whispers tickle the leaves up high,
As happy thoughts float on by.

Clouds bounce like children at play,
Frolicking softly in the day.
With each breeze comes a happy cheer,
Life's silly moments drawing near.

The sunkin creaks with a joyful creak,
As squirrels chatter with a little sneak.
Furry friends hold a comedy night,
In nature's theater, pure delight.

Every rustle, every little sound,
Hums a melody where joy is found.
So let your worries drift with the air,
In this whimsical world, strip down to bare.

Playful Secrets of the Arboreal

Among the branches, laughter rings,
Squirrels plot mischievous things.
With acorns flying through the air,
Nature's jesters in a dare.

The owls wink from their leafy thrones,
Sharing secrets in playful tones.
Branches sway with each silly word,
As the whispers can hardly be heard.

Lively shadows take a spin,
While the trees join in, grinning wide.
Every rustle a chuckling spark,
Creating joy in this verdant park.

So climb aboard the laughter train,
Where roots dig deep but spirits remain.
Among these trees, where fun is the rule,
You'll find the heart of nature's school.

The Lightness of Laughter

Jokes flip and swirl in the air,
As giddy winds dance without a care.
Tickled tongues and silly dreams,
Where every thought bursts at the seams.

Faces bright with beams of light,
Chasing shadows, pure delight.
Mirthful moments chase the frown,
In this joyful, carefree town.

Giggles echo through the green,
In this place, life feels a dream.
With each chuckle, spirits soar,
Who knew joy could open more?

Whispers of fun in leafy nooks,
Silly tales from storybooks.
Laughter blooms like flowers fine,
In the heart, where joy entwines.

Giggling in the Glade

In the glade, where jokers play,
Sunshine breaks the dullest day.
Sprightly jests and merry tunes,
Bouncing high like fluffy balloons.

Every leaf seems to partake,
In the giggles that we make.
Squirrels chuckle, birds retort,
Nature's playground, the finest sport.

With every step, a new delight,
Chasing shadows, feeling light.
Grins grow wide as laughter flows,
In a world where humor glows.

So join the fun, don't be shy,
Let your laughter reach the sky.
In the glade, we live and cheer,
Filling every heart with the sheer.

Swaying with Smiles

On the breeze, a gentle sway,
As smiles dance the clouds away.
Mirthful moments, pure and bright,
Painting skies with sheer delight.

Beneath the boughs, we share our glee,
Tickling thoughts as wild as the sea.
Who knew joy could leap this high,
As dreams take flight, we touch the sky.

Every whisper, a chuckling sound,
As joyful spirits swirl around.
With silly steps and twinkling eyes,
In this realm, the laughter flies.

So let us leap and let us twirl,
In the magic of this swirl.
Every giggle spins a tale,
In the breeze, where smiles prevail.

Cheerful Shadows of the Trees

Under canopies, laughter rings,
In the shade, the joy it brings.
Playful breezes, soft and kind,
In cheerful shadows, life's designed.

Watch the critters join the fun,
Chasing beams from the warming sun.
Little whispers full of cheer,
In every nook, the joy is clear.

Dancing leaves with vibrant tones,
Bringing life to sunlit zones.
Every shadow hides a grin,
Where giggles swirl, we feel the spin.

So gather here, forget your woes,
In this space where laughter grows.
With every step and every glee,
We paint the world so joyfully.

Buffoonery Beneath the Boughs

Beneath the green and leafy shade,
Clowns and jesters dance and parade.
With oversized shoes and bright red noses,
They tell silly tales as laughter dozes.

Squirrels giggle, and rabbits cheer,
As giggles stretch from ear to ear.
Twirling about, the shadows prance,
In this woodland, no one stands a chance.

Tickling trees with a playful tease,
While branches nod with effortless ease.
Frogs in top hats leap and croak,
As if the woods are all one big joke.

So if you wander where the giggles bloom,
Join the merriment, dispel your gloom.
For under these boughs, our hearts shall lift,
In the absurdity, lies a delightful gift.

Jolly Journeys Through the Leaves

Wandering paths where laughter flows,
Under the sun, where mischief grows.
A duck with a top hat, quite absurd,
Quacks quips and jests, spreading the word.

With every step, the shadows dance,
As squirrels chase their nutty romance.
Twirling with joy, in a whirl of greens,
Jumping over roots like playful machines.

Leafy confetti falls from above,
As friends giggle and share some love.
A songbird sings from a branch so high,
Its melodies melt like the clouds in the sky.

In this woodland adventure, come along!
Where whimsy reigns, and all is song.
Through leafy trails where spirits rise,
The joy of the journey is our constant prize.

Vine-Draped Revelations

Amidst thick vines, our secrets creep,
Whispers of jest as we gather and leap.
Twinkling eyes under canopies bright,
With every chuckle, we claim the night.

A raccoon in shades shares tales of the day,
Of shiny goblets and treasures at play.
Giggling flowers sway in the breeze,
As shadows weave magic through rustling leaves.

With every twist and every turn,
We find joy in the tricks and the burns.
Like tangled vines, our laughter entwines,
In this garden of whimsy where everyone shines.

So grab a friend, and share the delight,
In the weave of the vines, we dance through the night.
For here in the tangle, we jest and we play,
Creating new wonders with every array.

Nurtured by Nectar and Nonsense

Sweet sipping nectar drips from the blooms,
A fuzzy bee hums in jubilant rooms.
With honeycombs stacked, and laughter in pair,
They summon the joy that dances in air.

Amid sticky antics, the critters convene,
Sipping the nectar, bright and serene.
A raccoon with a straw drinks up all the fun,
While ants form a line, seeking nectar's run.

They twirl and they spin in a vibrant haze,
Celebrating silliness in endless ways.
Beneath the blossoms, the giggles ignite,
Creating a symphony of pure delight.

In gardens of nonsense where joy is the rule,
Every moment is precious, every chuckle a jewel.
So join us here, where the nectar flows free,
In a banquet of laughter, come share it with me.

Chuckles in the Canopy

In the trees where the squirrels play,
A parrot tells jokes all day.
Leaves shake with glee, what a sight,
Laughter echoes, taking flight.

Beneath the boughs, shadows prance,
The moon, it winks, in a funny dance.
Acorns drop with a soft thud,
While branches sway in a playful flood.

Birds chirp in the silliest tone,
To tickle the funny bones alone.
While wise old owls hoot with flair,
Sharing puns that fill the air.

In the canopy, joy abounds,
Where humor lives, and laughter sounds.
Oh, what a merry, jolly spree,
In the quilt of green, wild and free.

Jests Among the Foliage

Beneath the leaves, the foxes play,
Trading quips in the light of day.
A hedgehog tells tales of old,
With humor rich, and a heart bold.

In every nook, a chuckle flares,
The insects join in, no one cares.
With blooms that giggle, petals sway,
Their fragrance brightens the sunny display.

A raccoon flips through his comic stash,
Cracking jokes in a tranquil splash.
Leaves rustle as if they laugh,
At the silly antics, the forest's calf.

In green retreats where smiles convene,
Joyful whispers in shades of green.
Life rolls on with cozy cheer,
Among the foliage, happiness near.

Rustic Revelries in the Shade

Beneath the trees, the laughter flies,
As fireflies sparkle and surprise.
Barrels roll with a raucous cheer,
With good-natured pranks and no fear.

Picnics set with yummy treats,
Whispers and chuckles, warmth that greets.
Old dogs nap with a knowing grin,
While cats roll with laughter within.

Joys abound in the gentle breeze,
With every rustle, the heart feels ease.
Silly games with pies and a race,
Cheeks smeared with cream, the silliest face.

In rustic corners, warmth abides,
With laughter echoing, love resides.
A world alive with stories spun,
In cozy shades, we all are one.

Giggles in the Garden's Embrace

In the garden where the daisies twirl,
A playful rabbit gives a whirl.
With blossoms bright and sunshine bold,
The tales they weave are treasures untold.

Butterflies giggle as they chase,
A buzz of joy fills the space.
The daisies nod with a smile so wide,
Creating giggles as they glide.

In every petal, a giggle blooms,
As sunlight dances between the rooms.
With frogs in concert, a charming show,
Their croaks keep time in a steady flow.

In this haven where laughter grows,
The heart finds peace, true joy flows.
With nature's voice, a symphony plays,
In the sweet embrace of sunny days.

Nature's Comedy under the Sky

The squirrel wears a tiny cap,
And steals the birdseed without a tap.
The daisies dance in shivery glee,
While caterpillars join in harmony.

A bee buzzes by, all dressed in gold,
Belly flopping, stories to be told.
The trees chuckle as branches sway,
Tickling sunshine, brightening the day.

A rabbit slips in a patch of mud,
Playing tag with raindrops, oh what a thud!
The world is bright with joyful prance,
As nature puts on its funny dance.

And under clouds that poke and tease,
Laughter ripples through the leaves and breeze.
This merry stage, so wide and free,
Nature's jesters, what a sight to see!

Rhapsody of the Roaming Breeze

The wind plays tricks upon the trees,
Tickling branches like carefree bees.
A kite gets caught in a friendly brawl,
    Dancing around, it takes a fall.

A raccoon flips pancakes on a stone,
  Wearing a chef's hat, all on its own.
The clouds throw shadows, just to play,
Making grass monsters dance and sway.

A fox in socks spills juice on his paws,
    Laughing at nature's funny flaws.
The brook sings songs of silly streams,
As fish jump out to chase their dreams.

Giggles echo through fields of gold,
  Memories crafted, laughter bold.
    With every gust, a jest is spun,
This merry rhapsody has just begun!

Whimsy in the Woodland

In a grove where shadows twist and glide,
   A hedgehog wears a hat, full of pride.
  The rabbits play cards beneath the trees,
     Sipping on dew from breezy leaves.

A woodchuck shout from its burrow deep,
"Who signed me up for this game of leap?"
And nearby, mushrooms gossip and sway,
    Spreading tales of the night and day.

   The owls chuckle, wise and bright,
At antics unfolding under the moonlight.
   A fox chases butterflies with grace,
But ends up tangled in a flowered lace.

With each rustle and every slight sound,
  There's humor sprouting all around.
In this woodland, where whimsy thrives,
    Nature's laughter keeps us alive!

Delights of the Rustic Retreat

Atop a hill, the goats are bleating
While birds offer an off-key greeting.
A pig in mud spins stories anew,
Sharing secrets about the dew.

The farmhouse creeks in an old ballet,
Chickens waltz in a plucky display.
Farmers stumble, corn kernels fly,
Around and round, oh my, oh my!

Mice nibble cheese in a corner nook,
Plotting escapes like a mystery book.
The sun sets low with a golden flick,
As crickets chirp their happy tick.

With laughter braided through every thread,
Rustic retreats, where fun is spread.
Here in the fields, life's joys are sweet,
In every moment, humor and beats!

Satire in the Sundrenched Skies

With a wink, the clouds conspire,
To tickle sunbeams, they retire.
A breeze that giggles, floaty and light,
Chasing shadows, a playful sight.

Gaily the trees sway to the jest,
As squirrels dive in a frisky quest.
The sun paints laughter on fields of gold,
In this realm where joy unfolds.

Frogs leap high with quirky ease,
Spinning tales in the rustling leaves.
While daisies dance in the vibrant air,
In a carnival of mirth, beyond compare.

So let the breezes carry our grin,
In this sunlit dream where giggles begin.
Every moment draped in delight,
A festive spirit, oh what a flight!

Dancing Dreams Among the Daisies

Whispers of flowers, secrets they keep,
Bumbling bees enter, a playful sweep.
Each petal pirouettes in the warm sun,
A joyous ballet, oh what fun!

Butterflies gossip in colors so bright,
Telling stories of day and night.
Daisies crown the jiving air,
While nature chuckles without a care.

With every breeze, a jig starts to swell,
In this meadow, all is well.
Frolicsome breezes weave through the grass,
In a frothy rhythm, as time flies past.

Let's join the revel, let spirits beam,
In this patch of sunshine, we slip into a dream.
With laughter ringing in every cheer,
Amidst these daisies, joy's crystal clear!

Larks and Laughter by Moonlight

Under the gaze of the giggling moon,
Larks serenade, a whimsical tune.
Stars wink playfully, shimmering bright,
As shadows dance in the silvery light.

With sprites and fairies, all in a row,
They trade silly secrets, setting the glow.
Each sound a riddle, each chuckle a tease,
In this midnight realm, hearts find ease.

The soft grass whispers beneath our feet,
As we sway with the night, feeling the beat.
Giggles echo through the cool, sweet air,
A tapestry woven with laughter and care.

Come gather 'round, let's banter and play,
In this luminous night, let worries stray.
The moon a witness to mirth so divine,
In the embrace of night, we brightly shine!

Sunkissed Smirks of Serenity

Beneath the sun's bright, cheeky glow,
Painted smiles scatter, a joyous show.
Rippling waves join the silver laughter,
Echoing softly, like a happy ever after.

With each gentle wave, secrets exchange,
A world of wonder, never strange.
Children giggle with splashes and yells,
In this paradise where joy dwells.

The sunbeams tickle the cheeks of time,
As crickets hum along to the rhyme.
Each shadow holds a secret smile,
In this paradise, let's linger a while.

So here we bask in the warmth so sweet,
With every heartbeat, we dance to the beat.
In sunnyside moments, our spirits soar high,
With playful smirks, we greet the sky!

Merriment in the Meandering

A squirrel wears a tiny hat,
Running circles, oh so sprat.
He tumbles with a chuckle loud,
Joining in the dancing crowd.

With a skip and silly grin,
Friends gather, let the fun begin.
Jumpy frogs on lily pads,
Quacking jokes, no room for sads.

The butterflies all chase their tails,
Telling tales of funny fails.
In the porridge of the stream,
Even fishies start to beam.

As daylight dims, their giggles rise,
Echoing amidst the trees that prize.
Underneath the painted skies,
Come join the fun, and surely, you'll rise!

Sun-Drenched Stories of Delight

Puppies leap and twist in sun,
Chasing shadows 'round for fun.
Each tumble brings a merry cheer,
As they bark, their joy is clear.

A game of tag on sandy shores,
Building castles, dodging roars.
Seagulls swoop with a clever jest,
While sunburned cheeks remain blessed.

Laughter trails like waves on sand,
Tickling toes on every hand.
A hammock swings with giggly sounds,
Where stories of the day resound.

As stars emerge in velvet night,
They whisper tales of pure delight.
And dreams arise, both big and small,
In joy's embrace, we all stand tall!

When the Forest Speaks in Smiles

In a grove where whispers blend,
Trees share secrets, laughter sends.
A rabbit dons a bright bow tie,
As foxes poke their heads to spy.

Chipmunks chatter, gossip flowing,
Allies in the fun, they're glowing.
Underneath a twinkling bough,
Napping logs hide laughter's vow.

A nearby mushroom tells a tale,
Of fairies riding on a snail.
With every giggle, roots do sway,
As nature joins the playful play.

When twilight brings a peaceful sigh,
The forest hums a lullaby.
Each tree, a friend, with stories spun,
In cheerful hues, our hearts outrun!

Merry Melodies from the Earth

Bouncing bunnies hop along,
To the rhythm of the song.
The daisies sway, in tune they dance,
Inviting all to join the prance.

A chorus of crickets fills the air,
With chirpy jokes that all can share.
Nearby, a ladybug plays drum,
As ants march forth, they're never glum.

In a patch where sunflowers sway,
A gentle breeze begins to play.
It whispers sweet, forever bright,
Bringing joy from morn to night.

So toss your worries, let them fly,
Underneath this vast, blue sky.
For in this realm, with spirits free,
Mirth and music are the key!

Rejoicing in the Garden's Glow

In the garden blooms so bright,
Petals dance in morning light.
Bees are buzzing, flowers sway,
Nature joins the lively play.

Laughter echoes through the trees,
Gentle whispers in the breeze.
Even frogs in ponds around,
Croak in rhythm, joy unbound.

Colorful creatures jump and spin,
Chasing sunlight, pure and thin.
Every inch, pure bliss contained,
In this world, delight is gained.

Joyful souls beneath the sky,
Catching moments as they fly.
With each bloom, a giggle grows,
In the garden, laughter flows.

The Essence of Cheer in Nature's Reach

Chirping birds sing songs of cheer,
Nature's chorus, loud and clear.
Sunny rays through branches peep,
In this realm, our spirits leap.

Squirrels juggling acorns high,
Making mischief as they fly.
Every rustle, every sound,
Brings a smile, joy profound.

Dancing shadows under trees,
Whirling leaves with playful ease.
Joyful moments, bright and quick,
In the heart, their magic sticks.

With each step, the laughter sings,
Nature shares its lightest things.
Joyful hearts beneath the sun,
In this haven, life's pure fun.

Whispers of Willow Winks

Willows whisper with delight,
Branches swaying, soft and light.
Overhead, the sky so wide,
Breezes carry joy and pride.

Mice in coats of gray do play,
Underneath the sunlit ray.
Every rustle, giggles swell,
In this place, all is well.

Butterflies, like dancers, twirl,
Colorful wings in a whirl.
Nature's jesters, flaunting hues,
Bring us smiles, and nothing blues.

Among the reeds, frogs in tune,
Croaking softly, always June.
With each sound, a laugh to share,
In the garden, joy is rare.

Glee Beneath the Green

Underneath the leafy shade,
Playful spirits never fade.
Children's laughter rings so free,
In the glade, what joy we see!

Giggling rabbits hops about,
Nature's fun, without a doubt.
Every flower waves hello,
In this place, pure joy does grow.

Clouds like cotton, drifting slow,
Casting shadows down below.
With each chase through dappled light,
Glee erupts, hearts feel so bright.

Joyful echoes fill the air,
In this haven, nothing rare.
Beneath the green, we celebrate,
Nature's laughter, oh so great!

Nature's Naughty Nods

The squirrel wears a tiny crown,
While birds gossip, never frown.
A frog leaps high in jester's glee,
Chasing bugs with raucous spree.

The flowers giggle in the breeze,
Tickling bees with fragrant tease.
A butterfly dons polka dots,
In this world of silly plots.

Breezes dance on sunny days,
While shadows play in playful ways.
A tree leans close to share a joke,
As acorns drop and giggles soak.

Each rustle holds a whispered pun,
In the woods where joy has fun.
And laughter echoes, soft and bold,
In the tales that nature told.

Uproarious Whispers of the Wood

A raccoon pranks the sleeping sun,
Stealing snacks—oh, what a run!
Owls hoot secrets from the night,
While fireflies twinkle, pure delight.

The brook chuckles as it flows,
With splashes bright from silly toes.
A hare hops high, then trips on air,
With laughter floating everywhere.

Tiptoeing through the swaying grass,
The wildflowers peek and pass.
Each twig and leaf has tales to share,
Of silly moments everywhere.

Laughter thrums like morning's tune,
With mischief thriving 'neath the moon.
In this forest where giggles grow,
Joyful whispers steal the show.

The Enchantment of Endless Laughter

The sun spills gold on soft, green grass,
As ducks go waddling—oh, what sass!
A fox in costume makes a scene,
With painted paws, a laughing machine.

The river sings a merry song,
Where pebbles dance and drift along.
A deer plays tag with shadows near,
While echoes ring with hearty cheer.

Clouds puff out like fluffy jesters,
Giving shade to playful testers.
What's that? A chipmunk's pirouette?
Nature's stage, a grand vignette.

Laughter sprinkles the morning dew,
With every breeze, a giggling hue.
Underneath the endless sky,
Life's a comedy that can't run dry.

Vines of Vigor and Vivacity

Through the vines, the laughter sways,
As playful monkeys steal the gaze.
Fluffy tails in mischief spin,
With wiggles, twirls, and cheeky grins.

The cherries blush with rosy hue,
As the wind carries whispers, too.
Each leaf shakes with a chortling sound,
In nature's theater, joy abounds.

Bouncing bumblebees declare,
A jesting dance in sunny air.
The sunlight sparkles every leaf,
With chuckles shared beyond belief.

And as dusk dons its velvet cape,
Laughter weaves a vibrant shape.
With each vine that seems to sway,
Nature shares its funny play.

Whispers of Joy in the Grove

Beneath the branches, giggles float,
Critters tell tales, on whimsy they gloat.
A squirrel doing dance, quite out of sight,
Mistaking its shadow for a friend in the light.

The breeze tells secrets, a tickle of cheer,
While blossoms chuckle, as if they can hear.
A deer stumbles back, startled by a sound,
Laughter erupts, all through the ground.

Frogs play the jesters, with croaks so absurd,
Bouncing and leaping, they're never deterred.
An owl rolls its eyes, in the depth of the night,
While the stars burst with giggles, a dazzling sight.

A picnic unfolds, with sandwiches singed,
Tomatoes flying, and lemonade hinged.
Music from nowhere fills the soft air,
Joy spreads like petals, without a care.

Echoes of Laughter Beneath the Leaves

Rustling leaves chuckle, in playful delight,
  As critters below scurry left and right.
  A rabbit hops high, then trips on a vine,
    Lands in a bush, looking quite divine.

Chirping birds whistle a melodious tease,
  Creating a symphony with the rustle of trees.
A fox dons a hat made of moss and of twine,
  Strutting through nature, a dapper design.

Bear cubs roll over, in a clumsy retreat,
  As puddles splash back with each unsteady feat.
  Giggles escape from the den by the stream,
Where dreams bounce alive like a light-hearted dream.

Morning dew glistens, a spark in the sun,
  With each tiny prism, the laughter is spun.
  Nature's own comedy, playful and free,
  Brings joy to the heart—just like a key.

The Humor of Hidden Nooks

In the nooks of the forest, surprises abound,
Where mushrooms wear hats, and owls twirl around.
A chipmunk with style, in spectacles bright,
Reads tiny funny books, under the moonlight.

Gnarled roots giggle, as they wiggle and sway,
As breezes make whispers, both cheeky and gay.
The shadows play tricks, making faces so round,
Each twist and each turn, brings delight to the ground.

A hedgehog does stand-up, with quills all askew,
Telling bold jokes that make daisies dew.
While frogs in tuxedos, serenade from afar,
Sharing punchlines under—an old twinkling star.

The crickets, they chirp, in comedic delight,
Joining the jesters of day turned to night.
Nature's own jest, with its humor and glee,
Invites us to dance, wild and free.

Merriment Amidst the Greenery

Amidst the green tangle, laughter takes flight,
As pixies engage in their sprightly twilight.
They twirl through the branches, with glittering cheer,
While the shadows of twilight invite all to near.

The mushrooms do giggle, in colors so bold,
As secrets are whispered, the stories unfold.
Squirrels share pranks, with acorns on hand,
Building a tower, as small as it's grand.

The brook joins the chorus, with splashes of fun,
While daisies pop up for a dance in the sun.
A butterfly flits, wearing a smile so bright,
Bringing moments of joy, pure and light.

In meadows of green, the joy can be found,
With laughter and mirth springing up from the ground.
Let nature's own whimsy lead you along,
To a world overhead, where the heart sings its song.

Whimsy Amongst the Wildflowers

In fields where daisies sway and spin,
A butterfly tumbles, a dance to begin.
With giggles of grasshoppers leaping about,
The sunbeams chuckle, there's joy, no doubt.

A bumblebee buzzes, wearing a crown,
As petals whisper secrets, never a frown.
The daisies are spouting their jokes, oh so bright,
While ladybugs laugh in pure delight.

The rabbits throw parties, a hop and a swipe,
Each thump of a foot is a punchline type.
With twirls and spins, the flowers join in,
What whimsy unfolds where the laughter can win.

Beneath a bold sky, the rainbow takes flight,
Colors collide, such a marvelous sight.
In the garden of giggles, peace reigns supreme,
A symphony of chuckles, a dreamer's big dream.

Heartfelt Hilarity in the Hearth

By the warmth of the fire, the shadows do play,
With jokes swirling round like the smoke in the fray.
The cat on the mantle, gives a wink and a nod,
As legs of the table go 'thump' like a squad.

A grand feast is set, but the spoons start to jive,
The gravy boat dances, oh, what a surprise!
With laughter that bubbles, like stew in a pot,
Each chuckle erupts, oh, just look at them trot.

The dog rolls with mirth, in a blanket cocoon,
While cookies play tag with the spoons in the room.
The heart is a rhythm, a beat to the fun,
Where quips fill the air, like rays from the sun.

As night casts its cloak, the jokes gently soar,
Each bellyache chuckle, a heartfelt encore.
In this cozy embrace, with love scaling heights,
We find joy in the hearth, through the laughter of nights.

The Joyful Symphony of the Woods

In tangled green depths, the critters convene,
With whistles and chirps, a most playful scene.
Squirrels tell stories, a nutty delight,
While shadows like fairies amble through light.

A stream hums a tune, soft splashes of cheer,
With frogs in the chorus, their croaks loud and clear.
The owls hoot in rhythm, a wisecrack, a wink,
While crickets play fiddles, a vibrant sync.

The breeze joins the party, a soft, silly tune,
As branches do jiggle and flower petals swoon.
With every new note, nature dances along,
In this woodland concert, where each heart belongs.

Underneath the great sky, twinkling with grace,
The woods are a stage in this wild, raucous place.
Where laughter holds court, and joy spins around,
In every sweet whisper, adventure is found.

Solstice Smiles Among the Stars

When the sun dips low, and the fireflies glide,
The night wraps its blanket, a magical ride.
With twinkles and chuckles, the cosmos awake,
As the stars share a joke, they're hard to mistake.

The moon, wearing glasses, peers down with a grin,
While comets throw parties, let the fun begin!
Galaxies giggle, swirling high in the dark,
While meteors race with a spark to embark.

The owls flap their wings, catch the giggling breeze,
And laughter erupts from the rustling trees.
Each blink of the night sky is a wink in disguise,
As the universe chuckles beneath watchful eyes.

In this symphony bright, the night dances through,
With joy as the anthem, a chorus so true.
The hearts find their rhythm, amidst stardust's cheer,
In this vast, wondrous space, laughter echoes clear.

Serendipity Under Rustling Branches

In a grove where shadows play,
Squirrels chatter, not a delay.
The breeze teases with tickles bright,
Laughter echoes, pure delight.

Flowers wiggle, dance in rows,
Beneath the sun, where the river flows.
Each petal acts like a silly clown,
With giggles fluttering all around.

A rabbit hops, quite unaware,
Chasing butterflies without a care.
Nature whispers secrets, cheerfully,
As branches sway, they giggle with glee.

So we join in, sprung from the ground,
Finding joy, in laughter drowned.
In this magic, we feel so free,
Beneath the branches, come dance with me.

The Jolly Dance of Nature's Bounty

In meadows bright, the daisies sway,
With every step, they shout hooray!
The sunbeams giggle on the green,
A lively dance, a joyful scene.

Ants in line, a marching band,
With tiny hats, they take a stand.
Grasshoppers leap and chirp a tune,
While shadows play beneath the moon.

Round the pond, the frogs all croak,
They share a joke, then start to soak.
The dragonflies twirl, a vibrant show,
As petals swirl in nature's glow.

With laughter weaving through the air,
Every creature joins in the fair.
In joyous frolic, we all partake,
In a dance that makes the heart awake.

Smiles Wrapped in Nature's Arms

A gentle breeze stirs up the glee,
As branches dance, wild and free.
The flowers laugh with colors bright,
Painting the world in pure delight.

The bumblebees buzz a silly song,
Wobbling their way, they hum along.
Butterflies play tag, a polka spree,
In this garden, joy's the key.

With every rustle, a chuckle shared,
In this dance, no one is scared.
The trees shake off their morning dew,
And join the fun, just like we do.

Nature wraps her arms so wide,
We tumble in, our hearts open wide.
In this wild embrace, we laugh and spin,
Finding magic in a life akin.

Frolics Beneath the Old Oak

Beneath the oak, with branches tall,
Squirrels leap, and leaves do call.
The ground is soft with laughter's echo,
Where every giggle starts to grow.

A hedgehog hides with a secret grin,
Watching friends play, where joy begins.
The sunlight dances on the grass,
As butterflies flit, making time pass.

The wind spins tales of antics grand,
While cricket bands strike up on command.
Gentle whispers, the breeze's jest,
In softest hearts, we all feel blessed.

Rolling through this grassy maze,
In nature's grip, we're lost in a daze.
With roots so deep and skies so wide,
We share the joy, the laughter, the ride.

Chirps and Chortles from the Thicket

In the thicket, chirps collide,
Jokes and giggles, side by side.
A squirrel giggles with a treat,
While birds drop tales, a funny feat.

The bushes quiver, all in mirth,
Each rustle teasing, full of worth.
A rabbit hops, it takes a bow,
With whiskers twitching, here and now.

A dance of shadows, swift and bright,
Laughter echoing through the night.
Crickets chirp a silly song,
In the thicket, where laughs belong.

With each rustle, joy takes flight,
Creatures twirl in pure delight.
The forest hums, a merry tune,
Underneath the smiling moon.

Frolicsome Breezes in the Bay

Waves are rolling, laughter flows,
Breezy whispers, funny prose.
Seagulls squawk with cheeky flair,
Telling secrets in the air.

Sandcastles, goofy and grand,
With seashells hiding on the sand.
A crab with jokes, it scuttles by,
Pinching laughter as it climbs high.

Kites are dancing, tails in knots,
Children giggling at funny spots.
Dolphins dive with playful grace,
Splashing joy in this safe place.

The sun sets down, a golden hue,
Smiles reflect in waters blue.
In the bay, where breezes play,
Funny moments light the way.

Grinning with the Gardener's Glee

In the garden, blooms abloom,
Laughter echoes, dispels the gloom.
A carrot wiggles, trying to hide,
As flowers pirouette, in joy they glide.

The gardener grins, with muddy hands,
Whistling tunes as the sunlight spans.
Weeds tickle toes, a playful tease,
As ladybugs dance upon the leaves.

With each sprout comes a silly face,
Nature's humor, a warm embrace.
Jumping beans giggling on the vine,
Tickling the toes with humor divine.

The harvest brings a joyous cheer,
As veggies laugh, and all draw near.
In every row, a chuckle thrives,
In the garden, where laughter thrives.

The Euphoria of Elms

Under elms where shadows dance,
Laughter swirls in a playful trance.
A squirrel juggles acorns with glee,
As branches sway to the rustling spree.

With every leaf, a story unfolds,
A tale of humor that never grows old.
A breeze whispers jokes, so light and free,
While the elms nod with a secrets' spree.

Picnics bust with happiness bright,
Sandwiches chuckle in the golden light.
A frisbee zooms, and a giggle soars,
As children play on nature's floors.

The sun dips low, painting the scene,
Joy and laughter, forever keen.
In the embrace of mighty trees,
Euphoria thrives on the gentle breeze.

www.ingramcontent.com/pod-product-compliance
Lightning Source LLC
Chambersburg PA
CBHW051637160426
43209CB00004B/684